IMAGES
of Rail

SPOKANE INTERNATIONAL RAILWAY

Mining and railroad magnate Daniel Chase Corbin contributed much to the growth and prosperity of Spokane and the Inland Empire. (Author's collection.)

ON THE COVER: This eastbound freight heads up the one-percent grade near Moyie Springs, Idaho, a favorite spot for renowned Spokane International photographer Larry Shawver. He stated, "Nothing could compare with the sight, sound and good mountain railroading in a lonely and beautiful setting." (Larry Shawver photograph, Jerry Quinn collection.)

IMAGES
of Rail

SPOKANE INTERNATIONAL RAILWAY

Dale W. Jones

Copyright © 2019 by Dale W. Jones
ISBN 978-1-4671-0299-5

Published by Arcadia Publishing
Charleston, South Carolina

Library of Congress Control Number: 2019930751

For all general information, please contact Arcadia Publishing:
Telephone 843-853-2070
Fax 843-853-0044
E-mail sales@arcadiapublishing.com
For customer service and orders:
Toll-Free 1-888-313-2665

Visit us on the Internet at www.arcadiapublishing.com

For Larry Shawver—the photographs he gave us keep the spirit of the Spokane International Railway alive.

Contents

	Acknowledgments	6
	Introduction	7
1.	Spokane	9
2.	MP1 to MP25	19
3.	Timber, Troops, and Hoodoos	33
4.	Sandpoint	47
5.	Shiloh	61
6.	Bonners Ferry	77
7.	Mountains and Tunnels	91
8.	Larry Shawver	109

ACKNOWLEDGMENTS

As a young railfan, I was fascinated by the sight of the colorful red-and-black diesels with the yellow stripes and unique "$" logo. This pictorial Spokane International Railway story would not have been possible were there not several photographers who generously contributed photographs from their collections. The lion's share of images in the book are courtesy of Pacific Northwest railroad historian and master model railroad builder Gerald "Jerry" Quinn, including scores of eight-by-ten, black-and-white Larry Shawver Spokane International prints. Listed alphabetically are additional photographers and researchers who participated in the project: Tom Burg, Alan Burns, Paul Clegg, Ted Curphey, Dorothy Dahlgren, Teresa Dyck, Jim Forte, Mike Forster, Tom Hillebrant, Bob Kelly and the staff at the Pacific Northwest Rail Archive, Tom Kreutz (a contemporary of SI photographer Larry Shawver), Harley Kuehl, Rick Kunz, Bill Linley, Charles Mutschler, Sheldon Perry, Denee Renouf, John Riddell, Frank Scheer, Mark Simpson, Robert Thompson, Scott Whitney, and Richard Yaremko.

Heartfelt thanks to my wife, Bonnie, for her unfailing support throughout the years, and to the staff at Arcadia Publishing/The History Press for giving me the opportunity to write this book on the Spokane International Railway.

After researching and accumulating railroad memorabilia for nearly 50 years, I have collected many images from original photographers, online groups, swap meets, and other sources. Unfortunately, many images have been passed around, with the original owner's identity becoming lost. A case in point involves prints made by Larry Shawver and others; many times, photographers printed several "originals" now residing in various collections. Notable is the Walt Ainsworth estate, with an accumulation of over 10,000 prints. One historian commented that Ainsworth rarely took photographs but was a prolific collector. Though they are not necessarily Walt Ainsworth originals, his name is on hundreds of prints and he rightly merits credit for saving thousands of Pacific Northwest railroad photographs. If I have used your photograph without proper credit, it was unintentional.

Unless otherwise noted, all images are Larry Shawver photographs from the Jerry Quinn collection.

Introduction

The last half of the 19th century was typified by tycoons and shrewd railroad barons. When the Civil War ended, factories built by the Union to defeat the Confederacy were retooled for peacetime industry. In the decades of the 1870s and 1880s, railroad mileage rose from about 35,000 miles in 1865 to over 163,000 in 1890. Moguls of the time realized that owning and building railroads could reap huge profits for their investments. Expansion of rail lines began on the East Coast and progressed toward the West as the 19th century ended.

Although not directly involved, a key figure in the development of the Spokane International Railway was James Jerome Hill, or simply Jim Hill. Spokane businessmen were eager to have an alternative shipping option to Hill's Great Northern and Northern Pacific Railroads and viewed him a tyrant with unwelcome monopolies in northeastern Washington and the Idaho panhandle. One cattleman described Hill as "the barbed-wire, shaggy-headed, one-eyed old son-of-a-bitch of Western railroading."

J.J. Hill's connection with rail transportation began in the late 1870s when the St. Paul & Pacific Railroad (St.P&P) and other Minnesota based railroads became insolvent. Hill examined the potential for profit by acquiring control of these rail lines. In May 1879, he partnered with George Stephen, Norman Kittson, and others to form a new railroad—the St. Paul, Minneapolis and Manitoba Railway (St.PM&M). Jim Hill set his sights on connections with the Canadian Pacific Railway (CPR) at Winnipeg, Manitoba. By linking the newly formed Canadian Pacific with his American routes, Hill envisioned a railroad route west without constructing an "all-Canadian route" along the rugged north shore of Lake Superior.

Jim Hill sought to hire men who had ambition and determination, and in 1881, he suggested that William Cornelius Van Horne be an officer of the railway. Van Horne had gained management skills while working on the Illinois Central Railroad and the Chicago & Alton Railway. In 1882, Van Horne strongly opposed Hill's plan of using US routings for the Canadian Pacific Railway and insisted on construction across the north shore of Lake Superior. This decision infuriated Hill, causing him to leave the CPR in May 1883, swearing revenge against Van Horne and the Canadian Pacific.

After returning to the United States, Hill began aggressive expansion of his Great Northern Railway, playing out a game of railroad chess across the northwestern states and southwestern Canada, building his own route to the Pacific and earning the title of "Empire Builder." Van Horne once described Hill as the "bitterest enemy Canadian interests have in the United States, and the most dangerous because he is the most unscrupulous." Hill built many rail lines that can be said served little function other than to make Canadian Pacific managers feel compelled to spend even more money in a foolish effort to counter him.

To thwart the advances of the Great Northern, Van Horne believed it was necessary for the CPR to build a rail line across the southern interior of British Columbia; sharing his view was Thomas Shaughnessy, who was to succeed Van Horne as the Canadian Pacific's president.

In 1897, work began building a southern route across the province from three different locations, but advancement was short-lived in view of the high cost of construction. To contain expenses, the CPR terminated the important Crowsnest Pass portion of the line on the south end of Kootenay Lake, cutting the road into three disconnected segments of track relying on boats to connect them. Despite the revenue generated by the mines in the region, there was no direct rail access to the rest of Canada, as these connections were now exclusively in the hands of Jim Hill. When Hill was forced out of the Canadian Pacific, he swore revenge, saying: "I'll get even with him [Van Horne] if I have to go to hell for it and shovel coal." It appears Hill's prophecy may have been fulfilled.

Enter Daniel Chase "D.C." Corbin, a new player in the western railroad scene who broke the Hill lines' stronghold in Washington and Idaho's "Inland Empire." Born in Newport, New Hampshire, on October 1, 1836, Corbin came west in 1855 as a government surveyor in Iowa and Nebraska before moving to Denver in 1862 and entering the wagon freighting business. By 1886, he had relocated to the Inland Empire and developed a combined rail and steamboat system connecting the mines in the Silver Valley of northern Idaho with the Northern Pacific (NP) main line east of Spokane, Washington—he ultimately sold these holdings to the NP in 1888. The following year, he became involved in the construction of the Spokane Falls & Northern (SF&N), and its subsidiaries the Nelson & Fort Sheppard and Columbia & Red Mountain Railways, linking Spokane to the mining and lumbering communities in northeastern Washington and southern British Columbia. In 1898, Corbin sold the SF&N system to the Northern Pacific, which was promptly resold to the Great Northern Railway. When Corbin sold the SF&N to Jim Hill, and all the papers were signed, he went up the SF&N line and took the telegraph lines down—poles, crossarms, insulators, and wire. Jim Hill said, "Hey you, I bought that railroad." Corbin replied, "You bought a railroad, you didn't buy a telegraph line." Purportedly, Corbin brought the poles and other equipment over and put them on his Spokane International Railway. It has been said he was the only man who ever beat Jim Hill.

Corbin invested in the Washington State Sugar Company at Waverly, Washington, the Spokane Valley Land & Water Company, the Corbin Coal & Coke Company, and the Eastern British Columbia Railway connecting to the Canadian Pacific Railway Crowsnest Pass route near Fernie, British Columbia.

The Spokane International Railway story is more than 1900s-vintage steam engines and colorful red-and-black first-generation Alco diesel locomotives. It's a mélange of home-built equipment, ties to unique logging and mining operations, and a contribution to supplying military needs of the United States and Canada during World War II. This pictorial story of the Spokane International Railway traces its international and local connections with every major railroad in the Pacific Northwest.

One

SPOKANE

The Spokane International Railway was a small, Class 1 railroad built in 1905 by D.C. Corbin as a 140-mile rail line from Spokane, Washington, to Eastport, Idaho. The "$" logo, seen here on caboose No. C-6, reflects the confidence that the railroad would be profitable interchanging traffic from the Canadian border to the Pacific Northwest, competing with James J. Hill's Great Northern/Northern Pacific railroads.

The Spokane International commenced construction in May 1905 but did not reach Spokane on its own rails until December 1906. Corbin faced many challenges securing a location for his passenger depot and used this 1907 Oregon Railway & Navigation (OR&N) station on the north side of the Spokane River near Division and Washington Streets until Spokane's Union Station was completed in 1914. (Jerry Quinn collection.)

As the Spokane International neared Spokane in 1905, local politics and influence by the Great Northern opposed Corbin's efforts to secure space for rail yard facilities. He was forced to lease land between the Spokane River and OR&N tracks. The OR&N depot is in the center background; note the Canadian Pacific boxcars in the foreground, indicating the CP's influence. (Jerry Quinn collection.)

Westbound Train No. 1 skirts the Spokane River near Erie Street on its way to Union Station. There are no visible shadows on the ground, indicating this scene is sometime after January 1931, when the arrival time into Spokane was changed from 8:00 in the evening to about high noon, at 11:50 a.m. (Walter Ainsworth collection, PNRArchive.org.)

The McGoldrick Lumber Company sawmill occupied about 80 acres along the Spokane River south of Gonzaga College and east of downtown Spokane. From about 1906 until a devastating fire in August 1945, the company was one of Spokane's largest employers, with added timber holdings around the region. The main sawmill in Spokane was accessed by the Union Pacific, Great Northern, and Spokane International. (Charles Libby photograph.)

The Union Pacific Railroad, under its predecessor the Oregon Railway & Navigation Company, entered the Spokane region in the late 1880s. The original OR&N/UP depot was the Spanish-styled building pictured on page 10. The Spokane International had direct access to this station after crossing the Spokane River near Gonzaga University. When the combination Union Station was completed in 1913–1914, a loop track was built connecting the SI near Napa Street while intersecting the Union Pacific, Northern Pacific, and Great Northern (Spokane, Coeur d'Alene & Palouse) lines, allowing Spokane International passenger trains entry to the new station. In the above image, SI Train No. 1 heads east in the late 1930s. Below, 40 years later in 1975, six Union Pacific diesels cross the same UP bridge over Trent Avenue. (Above, Jerry Quinn collection; below, Jerry Quinn.)

Union Pacific NW-2 No. 1071 pulls an Expo '74 passenger special west past Gonzaga University on original Spokane International tracks. The station facilities on the north side of the Spokane River near Washington Street had long been removed, but during the 1974 World's Fair, the railroad built temporary passenger car connections near the original OR&N/SI site for special events and dignitaries. (Jerry Quinn.)

In the early years of the 20th century, railroads were the driving force in the development of Spokane. Throughout the years, there has been one structure that has remained constant—the Schade Brewery opened by German immigrant Bernhardt Schade in 1903. His building, seen here, featured unique architectural designs from his homeland. (Jerry Quinn collection.)

After leaving N.P. Crossing, the Spokane International/Union Pacific headed west to access Union Station. At ground level, the Union Pacific and Spokane International entered downtown through a tunnel below ground level in the "trench." Above, Spokane International Train No. 1 has arrived from Canada at 11:50 a.m.; below, Milwaukee Road 2-6-2 "Prairie" No. 5636 switches a local industry. Note the silhouette of the Schade Brewery in the background. (Above, Charles Libby photograph; below, Walter Ainsworth collection, PNRArchive.org.)

The original OW&N station north of the Spokane River at Washington Street was in operation for seven years before the joint Oregon-Washington Railroad & Navigation and Chicago, Milwaukee & St. Paul Railway Union Station on Trent Avenue opened in September 1914. An agreement from 1915 allowed the SI trackage rights to the station and use of downtown sidings. Above, a Union Pacific passenger train exits one of two tunnels in a westward approach through the "trench" to Union Station. The lower grade track provided access to industry sidings under the Union Station viaduct. Below, Union Pacific passenger Train No. 67 heads toward Dishman, Washington, and east to Wallace, Idaho. Berg's Tent Factory building on Division Street, visible in both images, was a Spokane landmark for decades. (Above, Jerry Quinn.)

The Oregon, Railway & Navigation Company entered Spokane from the southeast in late 1889, building a combination OR&N and Great Northern station north of the Spokane River; this first "Union Station" was destroyed by fire in 1902. Above, the 1914 Union Station featured a large Milwaukee Road–Union Pacific–Spokane International Railway sign lit by red neon lights at night. The photograph below was taken shortly after completion and highlights the ornate but functional second-floor/track-level waiting room. The Spokane International Railway ended all rail service to Union Station in September 1954. (Above, Mike Forster collection; below, Charles Libby photograph.)

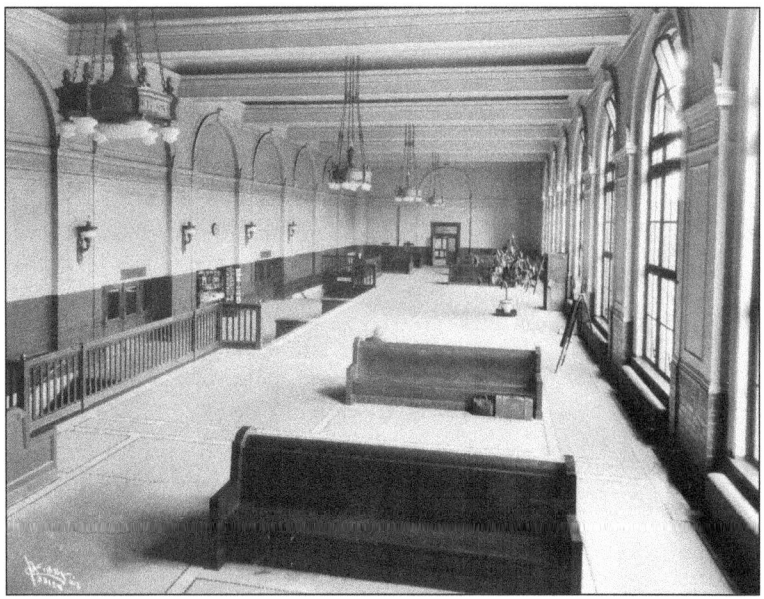

When the original 1889 combination Oregon, Railway & Navigation Railway and Great Northern depot burned, the new Great Northern station on Havermale Island was nearing completion. The prominent GN clocktower has overlooked downtown since 1902, and today the tower is a symbol for the city of Spokane. Above is a view looking west from the upper level of Union Station. The passenger cars in the foreground are located on a ground-level UP/MILW/SI Union Station connection near Washington Street. This track near the Union Pacific freight station was not used for regularly scheduled passenger trains; this may be a special train or cars waiting in storage. The postcard below features the northeast side of the recently completed Great Northern Railway station. (Above, Mike Forster collection; below, author's collection.)

Above, a Milwaukee Road 0-6-0 switches a freight car at street level near the industry tracks beneath Union Station. For many years, the noted Inland Empire photographer Charles Libby recorded the annual Sportsman's Show celebrating nature and outdoor recreation, held under the Union Station viaduct in downtown Spokane. The below photograph advertises "America's Greatest Outdoor Show – May 12 to 17, 1930" with a mounted white sturgeon. One reporter noted, "Ironically at the Sportsman's Show—devoted as it was to the outdoors—no attention was paid to the actual river beside the trestles." (Above, Mike Forster collection; below, Charles Libby photograph.)

Two

MP1 to MP25

Traditionally, railroads used milepost markers specifying locations along the line for track maintenance, hence the term "MP." This chapter begins at Spokane Shops or MP2.7, which is approximately two miles east of Union Station (MP1) and continues to Coeur d'Alene Junction at MP25.5. The Spokane International Railway's shops were equipped to maintain steam and diesel locomotives. Here, Alco RS-1 No. 204 gets a checkup.

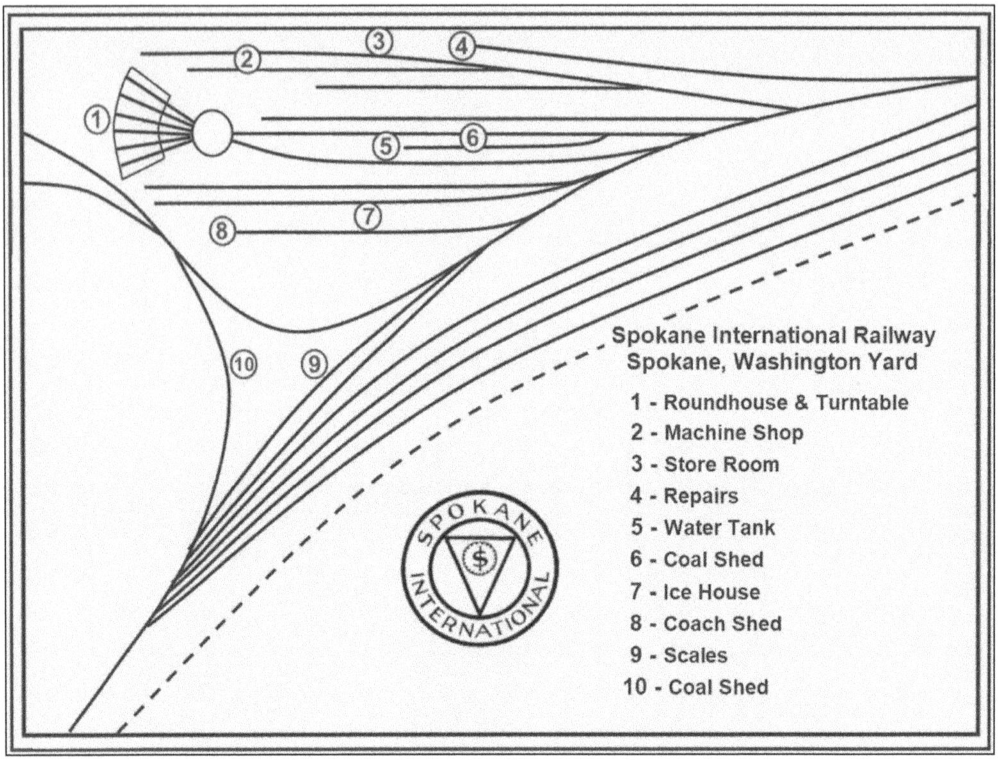
1
2
3
4
5
6
7
8
9
10
Spokane International Railway
Spokane, Washington Yard
1 - Roundhouse & Turntable
2 - Machine Shop
3 - Store Room
4 - Repairs
5 - Water Tank
6 - Coal Shed
7 - Ice House
8 - Coach Shed
9 - Scales
10 - Coal Shed
SPOKANE
INTERNATIONAL

The Spokane International shops were located at the corner of Mission Avenue and Greene Street; the map above identifies the position of buildings in the shop complex. In addition to numbered buildings, there was a 68-foot by 87-foot stockyard, a 14-foot by 28-foot sand house, a train order office, and a miscellany of other outbuildings. In the center is the four-track switching/staging yard, with a dotted line representing the Spokane, Coeur d'Alene & Palouse (Great Northern Railway) route to Coeur d'Alene. Below is an overview looking east at the shops; in the foreground, Alco RS-1 No. 200 is by the water tank amongst an assortment of maintenance buildings. (Above, Dale Jones.)

200

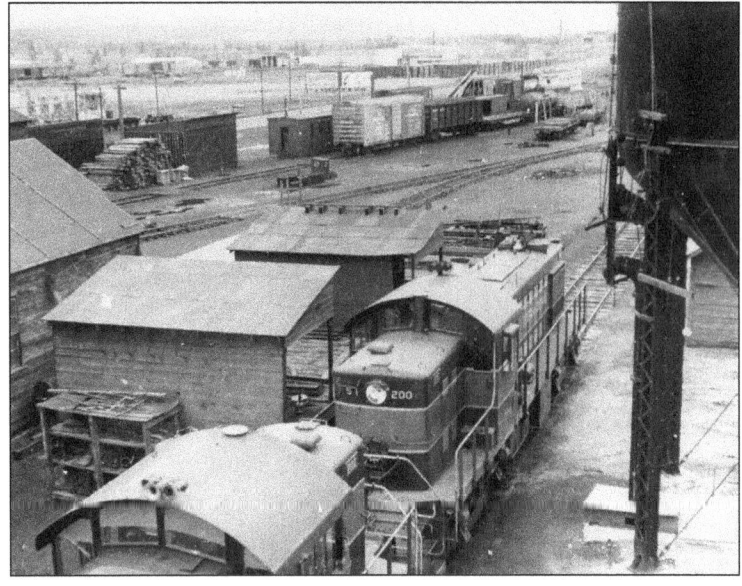

After the Union Pacific Railroad took control of the Spokane International in late 1958, the Alco RS-1s were quickly replaced by EMD "F" units. Above, No. 505 and two "B" units are near the coal dock at Spokane Yard. Diesel spotters may notice the lack of Farr-Air–style grills, indicating an F3 vintage; these units were equipped with internal components of EMD's F9 locomotives installed in retired F3 car-bodies. In the background is SI crane No. X-891, with two cabooses sitting on the coach shed track at right. Below, 30 years have passed from the time of the above photograph as a northbound freight passes beneath the Freya Way bridge snaking through the original four-track Spokane International switching yard. (Below, Jerry Quinn.)

The roundhouse's unique circular design was constructed around the turntable to easily and quickly turn locomotives. The only roundhouse on the SI was located at Spokane Yard; this 1907 structure typifies the most widely used design: clerestory roof, glass-pane doors, and chimneys to vent locomotive smoke. Originally, turntables were hand operated (hence the moniker "Armstrong"); but in the 1950s, the turntable pit was enlarged, with an electric motor installed for control. After steam engines vanished, the roundhouse was still used for diesel storage and repair. Below, the turntable accessed several short tracks for storage of M-O-W (maintenance-of-way) equipment; note weed-burning machine No. X-803 on the back track.

Coal docks, coal towers, or tipples were essential to the operation of steam locomotives and were generally built either next to or directly over the tracks. The primary Spokane International coal dock at Spokane Yard was located near the water tank. The photograph above shows the original 1907 coal dock that remained in service through the end of steam operations in 1949. Photographer Larry Shawver wrote on the back of this print, "By hand or by electric conveyor belt the railroads were glad to be rid of coal." Below, No. X895, built from flatcar No. 37, has a fragile-looking but functional pile-driving boom.

In the late 1890s, the US Post Office Department advertised seeking improvements in mail exchange devices. Ultimately, four common models were chosen: the Fleming, Ayers, Columbian, and Barker mail catchers. Spokane inventor Herbert E. Smith patented his own design on December 28, 1920. Frank Scheer, curator of the Railway Mail Service Library, explains, "Several inventors were attempting to develop a catch-and-dispatch device like the British design . . . the successful inventor would reap royalties from manufacturers selling the equipment to railroads. They usually worked with smaller railroads to demonstrate the operation to postal personnel. The demonstrations usually didn't have live mail." This train may be a trial run, as notes on the back of the print state, "This experimental mail pickup stand is on south edge of Felts Field in 1920." The Spokane International maintained a US Postal Service contract until around 1955. (Both, Jerry Quinn collection.)

Originally called Woodard, or Woodard Station, after the family that originally owned the land, this location became Millwood when the Inland Empire Paper Company mill was built in 1910. The photograph above shows a westbound Spokane International freight approaching the Millwood depot. The Great Northern (SC&P) Millwood station was directly south of the SI depot. When the mill opened, crews came to and from work on the train. The 3:45 p.m. whistle told them they had 15 minutes to catch the 4:00 p.m. train. The train no longer stops in Millwood, but a tradition of 7:00 a.m., 12:45 p.m., and afternoon steam whistles continues today. (Above, Tom Kreutz, Washington, Idaho & Montana Railway History Preservation Group collection; below, author's collection.)

In the 1920s, the Inland Empire Paper Company purchased Northern Pacific Class L-5 0-6-0 No. 924 and Class E-4 4-6-0 No. 388; the IEP re-lettered the tenders to its company name but left Northern Pacific markings on the locomotive cab. Photographs of No. 388 are uncommon, as it was retired around 1946. Above, the 4-6-0 pulls an empty gondola west from the log piles in December 1944. Below, No. 924 sits near the log pond in February 1947. After being retired from service, the 924 was stored on-site until shipped to the Northwest Railway Museum at Snoqualmie, Washington, in 1969. (Both, Tom Kreutz, Washington, Idaho & Montana Railway History Preservation Group collection.)

The Inland Empire Paper Company produced its own groundwood pulp from spruce and white pine trees. Here, in February 1947, No. 924 scuttles a load of pulpwood in the log yard east of the mill. On Saturday, September 7, 1957, a fire presumably started by the 924 destroyed 8 million board feet of logs valued at $400,000. (Tom Kreutz, Washington, Idaho & Montana Railway History Preservation Group collection.)

In 1905, the cement industry began on the Washington coast at Concrete, Washington; the first cement manufacturing facility in the Inland Empire region was International Portland Cement at Metaline Falls, Washington. In 1911, the International Portland Cement Company built this plant at Irvin, about two miles east of Millwood, with the Spokane International accessing the plant from tracks in the foreground and joining the Northern Pacific in the background. (Jerry Quinn collection.)

After the railroad's incorporation in 1905, the route for the Spokane International from Canada south was secured, but access into Spokane had not been firmly established. The line from the Idaho state line through Spokane Valley faced a crossing over the Spokane River at Trentwood and under the Northern Pacific at Woodward. A few weeks before the SI's first train on November 1, 1906, D.C. Corbin's dilemma was solved by temporarily running trains over the Spokane & Inland Empire electric line seen to the right of the westbound SI freight above. Below, Union Pacific GP38-2 No. 2025 leads an eastbound work train under the Northern Pacific (Burlington Northern) tracks at N.P. Subway—interestingly, no "subway" existed here, just the concrete bridges. (Above, Tom Kreutz, Washington, Idaho & Montana Railway History Preservation Group collection; below, Jerry Quinn.)

Above, looking west from the Sullivan Road overpass on a warm, sunny April 1977 afternoon, Union Pacific GP7 No. 100 shuttles cars on the Spokane International access tracks to Kaiser Aluminum's Trentwood rolling mill / fabrication facility. The US Government Defense Plant Corporation created the Trentwood facility in 1942 to produce aluminum for B-17 aircraft. In 1946, Kaiser leased the facility and later purchased the property. Between 1948 and 1963, the Spokane International moved 2,000 to 3,000 carloads of aluminum annually. Below, Trentwood-based local switcher GP38-2 No. 2009 waits as eastbound freight No. 8 with three SD40-2s passes an adjoining aluminum recycling plant in June 1979. (Both, Jerry Quinn.)

This crossing over the Spokane River at MP10.6 was assigned Bridge No. 1. Around 1949, the original 1906 structure was replaced with this steel-deck girder design. Above, a freight train heads west with a common locomotive consist from the mid-1970s, including three GP9B units sandwiched between two GP38-2s. Note: "GP" is a General Motors Electro Motive Division (EMD) designation for "general purpose." The passenger special below from September 13, 1975, is led by EMD "P," or passenger units—in this instance, E9A No. 960, built in 1950. The Union Pacific is one of the few modern US railroads that continues to maintain a fleet of heritage passenger equipment. (Both, Jerry Quinn.)

In 1886, the only connection south of the Northern Pacific main line at Hauser to Coeur d'Alene City, Idaho, was the Spokane Falls & Idaho Railway built by Daniel Corbin. This location eventually was named Grand Junction for three crisscrossing railroads. The above photograph from the 1950s shows the Northern Pacific line in the foreground: from left to right, the Spokane International crossing the NP up the middle; and since 1916, the Washington, Idaho & Northern (Milwaukee Road) veering off left to the north. When this scene was recorded, the SI Grand Junction depot was painted with bottom shingles green, white trim, and maroon siding. In 2019, only the Spokane International, now Union Pacific, and an infrequently traveled Burlington Northern Santa Fe branch (former Northern Pacific) line to Post Falls, Idaho, remain. (Below, Dale Jones.)

After Corbin completed the Spokane International Railway main line from Spokane to Canada, he built two branch lines accessing the lucrative timber and mining resources on Lake Coeur d'Alene and Lake Pend Oreille. The Coeur d'Alene and Pend d'Oreille [sic] Railway Company was incorporated in April 1910. It completed the 9.34-mile Coeur d'Alene section in April 1911. Here, Spokane International Alco RS-1 No. 208 and one of three former wooden Great Northern cabooses are turning on the wye near Sherman Park in Coeur d'Alene on a snowy February 1952 day. (Tom Kreutz, Washington, Idaho & Montana Railway History Preservation Group collection.)

Three

TIMBER, TROOPS AND HOODOOS

About 70 miles south of Eastport, Idaho, and the Canadian border, Spokane International westbound passenger Train No. 1 is passing through Dover, Idaho, at 9:26 a.m. on July 9, 1948. Locomotive No. 21, built by Alco for the SI in 1906, steamed until the diesels took over in late 1949.

After 1941, when the Calgary sleeper was eliminated, the normal consist of Spokane International passenger trains was one baggage/mail, one coach, and one smoker car. This photograph of Train No. 1 near Garwood, Idaho, shows an extra coach due to a Greyhound bus strike in March 1946.

For a brief time, the Idaho and Washington Northern Railroad chartered by lumberman mogul Fredrick Blackwell operated a six mile connection to the Spokane International between Coleman, Idaho, just north of Spirit Lake, and Clagstone, Idaho. This Marion Model 12 Loader, one of 20 built between 1906 and 1916, is working for the I&WN near Coleman. (Jerry Quinn collection.)

The Ohio Match Company purchased a large tract of timber from the US Forest Service in 1923 known as the "Lost Block." This virgin forest encompassed the Burnt Cabin Creek headwaters of the Little North Fork of Coeur d'Alene River. Prior to World War II, the principal method of lighting fires was wooden matches manufactured from western white pine. The logging railroad built to harvest this timber reportedly cost $1 million and connected with the Spokane International at Ohio Junction near Garwood, Idaho. To reach the 80 million board feet of virgin timber (that's a lot of matches!), the route took an easterly course across farmlands, meandering up the Hayden Creek drainage, twisting and turning for 20 miles and cresting at the 4,005-foot Burnt Cabin Summit. The final five miles of the main line descended 1,000 feet to the terminus where Bottom and Burnt Cabin Creeks meet. This photograph shows geared Heisler logging locomotive No. 2 on the rear of a loaded log train and Heisler No. 1 heading toward Burnt Cabin Summit. (Museum of North Idaho P-LOG-10-007.)

The Burnt Cabin Railroad operated the most common logging steam locomotives—the Shay, Climax, and Heisler. Pictured here is Ohio Match Heisler No. 4 laying rails in the Hayden Creek drainage. The Heisler was configured with two steam cylinders positioned in a "V" under the boiler. The piston rods came out of the cylinders and attached to a crankshaft drive powering the wheels. (Museum of North Idaho P-LOG-10-031.)

A crew of 50 workers rides a Spokane International flatcar being pushed uphill by Heisler No. 4 skirting the north flank of Deerfoot Ridge and crossing Two Forks Creek at Camp 11. "Camps" were designated by numbers corresponding to the mileposts along the line. Note the remnants of toothpick-like snags from the 1910 fires in the Mokins Creek drainage. (Museum of North Idaho P-LOG-10-057.)

As the track gang nears the Burnt Cabin Summit from the west, Mr. Ghebon, the crew foreman, operates the rail-bending machine located on the flatcar. This apparatus, designed by construction engineer Ray A. Biggs, was built to bend rails to any curvature as the work proceeded. The view in the photograph below looks southwest from Burnt Cabin Summit toward Hayden Lake. The Mokins Creek drainage is to the right, with Horse Ridge at center, dividing Mokins and Jim Creek on the left. Both images show the simple track-laying arrangement of spikes driven straight into untreated crossties without rail stabilizing tie plates. (Both, Museum of North Idaho; above, P-LOG-10-058; below, P-LOG-10-060.)

This fascinating gas-powered motorized Buda speeder built during the 1920s could carry 10 men on a five-percent grade with a 32-degree curvature. The photograph appears to show the east side of Burnt Cabin Summit in one of the cuts created from some of the 300,000 pounds of dynamite required to build the line. Construction began in July 1923 and was continuous, summer and winter, for more than a year, except for a two-day Christmas vacation. It must be a cool day, as the man on the right is wearing gloves and thick woolen socks inside his caulk boots; he may be construction engineer Ray A. Biggs, as he is wearing a dress shirt and necktie beneath the heavy flannel coat. (FS No. 192398, Museum of North Idaho P-LOG-10-052.)

The Spokane International was instrumental in providing support building the Alcan (Alaska) Highway during World War II. The attack on Pearl Harbor and Japanese occupation of the Aleutian Islands of Atta and Kiska accelerated the need to build a highway connection to Alaska. Construction began in March 1942 as trains moved hundreds of pieces of construction equipment and American troops to Dawson Creek, British Columbia, the northernmost stop on the Northern Alberta Railway. The SI ferried supply trains from Spokane to Eastport, Idaho / Yahk, British Columbia, with the Canadian Pacific completing the trip through Crowsnest Pass north through Fort MacLeod, Calgary, and Edmonton, terminating at Dawson Creek. In the above view, a bystander inspects a trainload of Chevrolet one-and-a-half-ton G7107 cargo trucks. Spokane International locomotive engineer Dewey Almas recalled, "Late in '42, we moved four trains of troops with five or six Pullmans for the soldiers and 15 to 25 cars of bulldozers, trucks and anything else." Below, US Army troops arrive in Dawson Creek. (Both, South Peace Historical Society Archives; above, 2000.067.007, below, 2000.051.017.)

This photograph from May 1943 highlights two interesting features of the Spokane International's contribution in building the Alaska Highway. No. 908 was one of four 2-8-0 locomotives bought secondhand from the Delaware & Hudson to augment increased traffic during World War II, and three cars back in this freight train are flatcars with truck trailers destined for Alcan construction. (Tom Kreutz, Washington, Idaho & Montana Railway History Preservation Group collection.)

Train No. 1 with No. 103 passes near Hoodoo Lake at Edgemere, Idaho, in November 1947. The Hoodoo Valley stretches from Garwood, Idaho, to the Pend Oreille River. A hoodoo can be a pointy rock spire (there are none nearby) or might be related to voodoo magic, perhaps a jinx. "Hoodoo Lakes" are cited on an 1874 US Army map. The source of the name remains a mystery.

All railroads require ballast or crushed rock to stabilize and maintain the roadbed. Ballast acts as a support base supplying strength and rigidity while allowing for flexibility and proper drainage of water away from the rails. One of the primary gravel pits on the Spokane International was located at Clagstone, Idaho. Both photographs were taken at the east end of Clagstone Pit, with Clagstone Ranch in the background. The above image shows eastbound Train No. 8 on a hot summer day with locomotive doors open to cool the diesel engines. The Union Pacific train seen below carries a company Instruction Car headed east in February 1961.

About five miles north of Edgemere, Idaho, the Spokane International leaves the Hoodoo Valley and parallels the Pend Oreille River east for 15 miles to Sandpoint. Both photographs were taken from John Fox's farm overpass near the S curves at Sawyer, Idaho. Locomotive No. 2000 above was one of three ex–Union Pacific 2-8-2 Mikados purchased in 1947 to supplant the four aging and unpopular Delaware & Hudson 2-8-0s acquired in 1943. Below is one of the early 4-6-0 locomotives bought by the SI in 1907; this engine was originally No. 24, rebuilt in 1926 and renumbered to No. 124.

The track profile along the Pend Oreille River between Colalla, Morton, Gravel Pit, and Dover, Idaho, is nearly constant at an elevation of 2,085 feet. At Morton, the Spokane International passes Morton Slough, an important breeding and brood-rearing locale for waterfowl. The photographer commented on the location: "This is typical of the land and farms down through the Hoodoo Valley." The above image shows Time Freight Train No. 15 near Sawyer, Idaho, on November 29, 1947—judging by the angle of the sun, this train led by 2-8-2 No. 1917 must be on time at 3:00 in the afternoon. Below, No. 1936 is framed in a classic three-quarter-angle pose with snow-covered mountains in the background and coal-fired locomotive smoke. This is a quintessential image of the Hoodoo Valley in 1949.

The long sweeping curve near Gravel Pit, Idaho, at MP68 was a favorite location for photographers to catch Spokane International westbound trains along the graceful Pend Oreille River. In the above view, from shortly after the Union Pacific takeover in July 1960, an EMD GP9, three F9 B-units, and a lone SI Alco RS-1 glide along Muskrat Lake. Below, photographer Larry Shawver's caption from July 6, 1948, reads, "Running fast – the No. 1936 moves #15 upgrade from Pend Oreille River near Gravel Pit – farther on the line will again drop down along river until it gets back to Morton, Idaho."

The Great Northern Railway built into Sandpoint and the north bank of the Pend Oreille River valley in 1892. This August 1953 scene shows an eastbound Great Northern Western Star No. 28 led by P7 No. 362C nearing the town of Priest River. On the south bank of the river is Sawyer, Idaho, on the Spokane International Railway. (Stan Styles photograph, author's collection.)

The Spokane International originally built three large wooden bridges: one spanning the Pend Oreille River at Dover, one at Sand Creek in Sandpoint, and the Kootenai River crossing at Bonners Ferry. These sparkling clean Union Pacific F9s pose on the new, shiny steel-girder bridge replacing the wooden trestle over the Pend Oreille River at Dover near completion in 1962.

After September 15, 1954, when the Spokane International Railway officially stopped running regularly scheduled passenger trains, photographs of passenger equipment on SI rails were a rare event. Interestingly, almost 41 years later to the day, this eastbound (northbound) Union Pacific *Director's Special* business train is crossing the Pend Oreille River at Dover, Idaho, on September 24, 1995. (Gary & Roz Miller, Jerry Quinn collection.)

After the SI crossing of the Pend Oreille River near Dover, both the Great Northern and Spokane International railroads paralleled each other into Sandpoint—so closely that the GN Dover depot had operator bays on both sides, one for the GN and one for the SI. On March 1, 1947, leased Northern Pacific No. 1592 leads freight No. 15 westbound through town.

Four

Sandpoint

Sandpoint, Idaho, is a crossroads for railroads and industry in northern Idaho. The Northern Pacific entered in 1882, with the Great Northern arriving in 1892. In the late 1890s, Jim Hill controlled both rail lines with a stranglehold on shipping rates. Sandpoint residents welcomed D.C. Corbin and the Spokane International connection in 1906. Here, No. 200 passes the iconic Lasswell Milling grain elevator around 1954.

As the original early 1900s locomotives began to age and train tonnage increased, the SI needed replacement motive power. Three 2-8-2 locomotives were purchased from the Union Pacific in March 1947. The added horsepower of these engines moved trains over the lesser grades like Shiloh and Pack River hills without a helper. No. 1936 waits in Sandpoint to head west.

During World War II, the 2-8-2's Mikados carried supplies in support of the war effort. In 1942, an attempt was made to change the Mikado name to one deemed more patriotic—MacArthur, in honor of Gen. Douglas MacArthur—but the new name never took hold. The three Union Pacific 2-8-2s retained their UP numbers; No. 2000 works one of the transfer tracks in Sandpoint.

The Spokane International utilized cabooses from diverse backgrounds. On July 12, 1956, two employees on caboose No. C-9 protect the train in a backup maneuver at Sandpoint. Cabooses Nos. C-9, C-10, and C-11 were former Great Northern Railway Nos. X577–X601 series 25-foot cabooses built around 1925. These GN "crummies" (slang for cabooses) were not well-liked by SI crews.

The circumstances surrounding the arrival of this train at the Sandpoint depot on a cool rainy spring day may be lost, but considering the interest of bystanders and locomotive crew, this may be something more than a required train order stop as indicated by the horizontal signal blade.

Above, the cover over the hood of the Ford Model A tells the story. A local resident recalls, "In February of 1936, we had 26 days that it never got above zero, usually 20 to 30 below or more and with the wind that was always blowing; the chill factor was terrific, as in those blizzards it would often blow 40 or 50 miles per hour." Below, an old Ford with license plate 7-B 949 indicates it was the 949th vehicle registered in Bonner County.

Establishing the dates of photographs can be a challenge, but it is usually possible to determine the era. This train is passing the original 1905 Sandpoint depot—a new station was built in 1962, Alco No. 203 was purchased in 1949, and a 1956 Plymouth Belvedere is pictured. It is reasonable to conclude that this photograph must be from the late 1950s. (Tom Kreutz, Washington, Idaho & Montana Railway History Preservation Group collection.)

Train No. 1 waits at the Sandpoint water tank. What keeps the water from freezing in the winter? The tank inside was round, with an open top. The octagonal exterior was a separate structure enclosing the tank with space for a stove that could be lit in winter to keep the interior temperature above, or at least closer to, the freezing point.

Following the discontinuation of passenger service in September 1954, the SI introduced a fast freight service. The two new trains, Nos. 8 and 9, included a combination baggage/mail car to maintain mail and express service. On a hot August 11, 1955, RS-1 No. 201 is operating with locomotive doors open for engine cooling and a trainload of British Columbia fruit.

Locomotive No. 908 was near the end of usefulness on the Spokane International when this photograph was taken at Sandpoint on May 4, 1946. The four Delaware & Hudson 2-8-0s purchased in 1943 had finished their intended purpose of support for increased wartime traffic and were soon retired and scrapped in 1947.

Train No. 1 with locomotive No. 25 leaves westbound Sandpoint on April 16, 1946. The photographer notes, "If a farmer had a can of cream to send to town, he would set it along the track and the train would stop and pick it up." The practice of picking up foodstuffs and dropping off orders from the grocery store continued until the train was cancelled.

Graffiti has become commonplace on railroad equipment in the 21st century, but doodles on trains were popular even during World War II, especially a bald man with prominent nose peeking over a wall featuring the inscription "Kilroy was here." In July 1949, a Spokane International employee drew his own doodle on No. 25 at Sandpoint.

Spokane International 4-6-0s Nos. 101, 102, 103, and 104 (original Nos. 1, 2, 3, and 4) were built in 1907. In 1925, No. 101 was rebuilt with larger cylinders, adding air through the firebox to the stack and reducing valve gear maintenance. Here, Train No. 1 heads west from Sandpoint to Spokane.

On July 8, 1948, Bill Miller, in the cab of No. 1936 eastbound, passes Train No. 1 at Sandpoint. Union Pacific 2-8-2s were equipped with a "doghouse" for the head brakemen; Spokane International rebuilt this particular former Union Pacific 2-8-2 tender for larger coal capacity.

At minus-16 degrees Fahrenheit after a big snow on New Year's Day 1949, No. 1936 pushes a Jordan Spreader snowplow westward near the junction of South Ella Avenue and US Highway 2 in Sandpoint. The Jordan Spreader, designed by Oswald F. Jordan in the 1890s, is simply an angled plow able to dig and clean ditches to regulate ballast and plow snow. There were two RS-1s (Nos. 200 and 201) outfitted for passenger service with a steam generator. The Spokane Shops added an automobile headlight mounted above the front number boards and attached a large wedge plow, a design that was unique to the Spokane International.

The war years brought a great deal of business to the Spokane International. After losing its Class 1 status in 1929, the SI saw the increased wartime traffic restore Class 1 status to the road, with revenues over $1 million a year. The original 1906–1907 vintage locomotives were operating at wartime capacity, with the SI having difficulty finding replacement locomotives. In April 1942, it settled for four heavily used and nearly worn-out 2-8-0s from the Delaware & Hudson. Nevertheless, these engines were the most powerful the SI owned. Above, in a snowy February 1946, No. 908 westbound blows hot cinders over Sandpoint just a short time before being scrapped in 1947. Below, on June 18, 1946, longtime Spokane International employee Dewey Almas oversees Extra 907 East between Sandpoint and the Sand Creek trestle.

Near the site of this spectacular trestle in 1809, explorer and surveyor David Thompson built a trading post, naming it a "pointe of sand." The original townsite, Sand Point, was located on the east side of Sand Creek. In the 1890s, the main businesses moved west across the creek, with the town's name changed to Sandpoint. This 660-foot structure built around 1905 spanned the slough between Sand Creek and Lake Pend Oreille. Located about 100 feet north of US Highway 2 at Sandpoint, the Sand Creek trestle was possibly the most photographed spot on the Spokane International. Here, two Union Pacific trains from the 1980s head west. The wooden trestle was removed and replaced by a nonflammable steel bridge in the 1990s, making the fire prevention water barrels obsolete. (Both, Jerry Quinn.)

Four of the twelve Alco RS-1s led by No. 211 approach the wye at MP76.2 where the Spokane International connected with the Northern Pacific at the location aptly named NP Ry Transfer. The SI had transfer tracks and agreements to interchange with both the Northern Pacific and the Great Northern at Sandpoint.

The Spokane International bought four new 4-6-0 passenger locomotives in 1906, numbered 1–4. In 1919–1920, they were renumbered with the addition of 100 to their running numbers. Here, No. 101, with westbound passenger Train No. 1, runs around leased Northern Pacific No. 1592 at about 9:20 a.m. near downtown Sandpoint.

In the post–World War II era, railroads were replacing aged and well-worn steam locomotives with diesel motive power. In April 1949, the Spokane International ordered nine 1,000-horsepower Alco RS-1 road switchers. Here, Nos. 202 and 203 from the 1949 order set out No. 209 from the 1953 acquisition on a Sandpoint depot track.

When the Spokane International took an engine out of service or needed supplementary power, it borrowed temporary substitutes from other railroads. These included CP 2-8-0 Class N-3 3900s, GN 4-6-0 Class-E 1000s, 2-8-0 Class-F 1100s, and 4-6-2 Class-H 1300s, along with Northern Pacific 2-8-2 Class-W No. 1592. In August 1942, CP 2-8-0 No. 3679 with Train No. 15 passes Train No. 14 at Sandpoint.

This handsome 1949 portrait of leased Northern Pacific 2-8-2 No. 1592 has engineer Hjalmer "Husky" Haaland waiting to "highball" a westbound extra freight at the Sandpoint depot and water tank. The Southern Pacific refrigerator cars may contain cherries or other soft fruits from the Central Kootenay region of British Columbia destined for southern markets.

Six 2-8-0s, Nos. 21–26, were delivered in 1906 to complete rail line construction. In August 1949, only months from retirement, No. 21 is leading westbound Train No. 1 away from the Sandpoint station on its way to Spokane.

Five

SHILOH

How did Shiloh get its name? One local historian noted, "I could never find out, as none of the old timers even knew the origin of the name themselves." On December 16, 1946, leased Northern Pacific No. 1592, along with No. 25, is pushing on the rear attack Shiloh Hill south (westbound) out of the Kootenai River valley between Bonners Ferry and Shiloh.

Diamond Match Company entered the northern Idaho timber / match block market in 1927 by building a narrow-gauge logging railroad at Priest Lake to salvage fire-killed trees. In 1931, the Priest Lake operations ended and locomotives Nos. 1 and 2 were standard-gauged. Diamond Match purchased timberland from Humbird Lumber Company in 1936 and built a 14-mile railroad in the Rapid Lightning Creek drainage. A new location on the Spokane International at MP79 was established and appropriately named Diamond Junction, near Sandpoint. The match company had a three-stall engine house, office headquarters, and a warehouse at the junction. Above in August 1943, No. 2 sits idle after the line had been abandoned; below, No. 4 is bringing logs up the Pack River Hill on a warm July 1940 day. (Above, Tom Kreutz, Washington, Idaho & Montana Railway History Preservation Group collection.)

Caboose No. C-3 tails an eastbound freight headed upgrade from Diamond Junction to Forest Siding. Nos. C-1, C-2, and C-3 were built by American Car & Foundry for the Spokane International around 1905. On this snowy January 1949 day, the 2-8-0 steam locomotive on the point has only about eight months of active service before retirement.

Former Union Pacific No. 2000 and two other 2-8-2s purchased in 1947 were the last steam locomotives acquired by the Spokane International. In the summer of 1949, engineer Tony Sciola leans out of the cab near Selle, Idaho. Selle was known as Matchwood until 1916 for the stands of white pine used to make matches.

The above scene has No. 201 leading an eastbound phosphate ore train past log gondolas set out at Forest Siding, Idaho. Phosphate is needed in the manufacture of fertilizer. During the 1930s, Cominco Ltd. developed a process that turned the phosphate-refining byproduct sulphuric acid and chalky phosphate ore into fertilizers marketed under the name Elephant Brand. The train load of hopper cars may appear empty, but a two-bay hopper half-full would contain the maximum weight of phosphate ore; this also explains the need for five locomotives. Below, unique to Nos. 200 and 201 is the conspicuous automobile-like headlight. Larry Shawver stated, "They were not like rotating Mars lights, but on-and-off non-rotating blinker lights; not anything like it today."

The folk saying goes, "If March comes in like a lion, it goes out like a lamb." Here, on March 2, 1947, the crew of leased NP No. 1592 on eastbound No. 14 switch cars in a spring snowstorm at Forest Siding, Idaho. By the next evening, 10 inches of snow would fall. Historical weather records indicate March went out like a lamb with a week of 50-degree temperatures.

The "station" at Grouse, Idaho, was nothing more than the shell of SI caboose No. C-4; in fact, the only way a train would stop was with the wave of a hanky or hat. Here, passenger Train No. 1 passes Grouse in August 1949. Larry Shawver's father, Truman (sitting) went to meet his school friend Ben Thompson (standing), who lived across the road from the station.

Most people love steam engines, and the conversion of water to steam is magic. To keep the beast rolling, there is much activity in the cab: the firebox must be fed, and an array of levers and gauges need to be controlled to get all that power to the rails. This image is a classic demonstration of the beauty of steam train operations in the dead of winter. Spokane International Class-F No. 1936 labors upgrade out of Samuels, Idaho, past Grouse, Idaho, on a double-digit below-zero day in January 1949. The winter of 1948–1949 was one of the most severe on record at that time. December 1948 saw four feet of snow followed by a month of bone-chilling 20-degrees Fahrenheit daytime average temperatures.

The Great Northern and Spokane International by and large paralleled each other between Bonners Ferry and Sandpoint. The two photographs on this page were taken at Elmira, Idaho. Above, Extra 1936 West takes the siding waiting for Train No. 1 to overtake and pass; below, caboose No. C-3 tails Extra 936 East while Train No. 1 with 2-8-0 No. 122 speeds by with white steam peeking through the smoke. During the 1930s, the SI and GN jointly studied the possibility of consolidating the two rail lines between Bonners Ferry and Sandpoint, eliminating what was essentially dual trackage. The proposal was scrapped, as it was agreed it would deprive the SI of its greatest source of online revenue.

Three Alco RS-1s led by No. 210 top Shiloh summit with a heavy eastbound phosphate ore train. Phosphate ore mined near Garrison, Montana, was destined for the smelters at Trail, British Columbia. The Northern Pacific and the Milwaukee Road both loaded ore for the Spokane International. The Milwaukee transported ore to Grand Junction, Idaho, for interchange with the SI, and the Northern Pacific interchanged with the Spokane International at Sandpoint.

On a bright summer day, former Union Pacific 2-8-2 No. 1936 heads up Shiloh Hill. Note the helper running in reverse, located two boxcars back in the train; the helper would be running backwards so it could drift back down the grade into Bonners Ferry facing forward, lessening the possibility of the tender derailing.

Mountain grades are the nemesis of railroads. The weight of freight cars and locomotives with smooth polished wheels riding on shiny steel rails is difficult to put in motion on level ground, more so as the slope steepens. Railroads employ several approaches to improve traction and augment available horsepower. The primary method of preventing wheel slip is by dispensing sand through tubes in front of the driver wheels. As the train increases speed, there is less friction to slow forward progress until it reaches an incline. To reach the summit, the engineer may simply pick up speed in advance, or the train can be double-headed by adding another locomotive before departure. In the past, some railroads utilized "mallets," articulated engines with two sets of driver wheels under one frame. Mallets could haul large tonnage without assistance but were labor-intensive to maintain. Smaller rail lines with modest grades like the Spokane International preferred to add helpers as needed or double-head, as with this westbound No. 15 with Nos. 1936 and 124 on Shiloh Hill in 1949.

In the event of a derailment, the Great Northern and Spokane International would detour on neighboring rails between Sandpoint and Bonners Ferry. The circumstances behind SI No. 207 and four other RS-1s bypassing on the Great Northern at Moravia, Idaho, is lost in time.

Is this locomotive No. 21 or No. 121? This engine was one of the six original 2-8-0 locomotives built as Nos. 21 through 26. Around 1927, Nos. 22, 24, and 26 were rebuilt and renumbered 122, 124, and 126. Some sources state that No. 21 was also renumbered. This photograph at Shiloh in 1949 confirms that No. 21 was never renumbered.

Following the end of passenger train service in September 1954, the SI introduced two new "Fast Freight" trains, Nos. 8 and 9, that maintained the US Mail contract with a baggage/mail car on the front of the train. This photograph of Nos. 201 and 205 leading Train No. 9 into the siding at Shiloh represents a typical mid-1955 train consist.

In 1907, Congress enacted the Railroad Hours of Service Act limiting railroad employees to shifts of 16 hours a day in any given 24-hour period. In August 1949, Train No. 2 left Spokane at 11:59 p.m., arriving in Yahk, British Columbia, at 5:50 a.m. and returning to Spokane at 12:02 p.m. This schedule was nearly exactly 12 hours. Bobby Brown, with No. 1 at Shiloh, has time to spare.

The photographer's notes for this image state, "No. 1917 gets Train 15 up to 60 mph before the hill gets steep." This is a former Union Pacific locomotive, and UP's timetables specified a maximum 80-miles-per-hour speed limit for steam engines. If the notes are correct, this train is traveling 15 miles per hour over the Spokane International systemwide 45-miles-per-hour speed restrictions and approaching maximum safe operating limits.

It is 86 degrees on a clear July 6, 1947, afternoon. Engines Nos. 2000 and 126 bring No. 15 up Shiloh Hill just north of Naples. The presence of the Jordan Spreader and a dozen gondola cars of rock directly behind No. 2000 indicate some right of-way work in the area was imminent.

Topping Shiloh Hill, a westbound freight with a string of empty gondolas led by No. 2000 heads back to interchange with the Northern Pacific at Sandpoint. After leaving Sandpoint, the train will go east on NP rails to the mines at Garrison, Montana, to be loaded with phosphate and returned to the Canadian Pacific at Curzon/Yahk—destined for Trail, British Columbia. (Walter Ainsworth collection, PNRArchive.org.)

In a dramatic cloud of coal smoke and with an imposing appendage called an Elesco feedwater heater, No. 122 attacks Shiloh Hill. A feedwater heater preheats water running through the smokebox before it is pumped into the boiler, significantly increasing steam engine efficiency.

The westbound passenger Train No. 1 passes an eastbound "in-the-hole" on the Shiloh siding between Sandpoint and Bonners Ferry. Note the "doghouse" on the tender of the 1917; railroads started using doghouses for the head brakemen, thus reducing the need to cross the coal pile of a stoker-equipped engine.

Naples, Idaho, is one of a few locations where the Great Northern and the Spokane International passed just feet apart. Here, Extra 2000 East leads a phosphate train loaded at Metaline Falls, Washington, or Garrison, Montana, to connect with the Canadian Pacific at Curzon/Yahk, British Columbia, for connections west to the Cominco smelters at Trail, British Columbia.

Engines Nos. 2000 and 126 bring Train No. 15 up Shiloh Hill just north of Naples. Number 126 is working as a helper on its way back to Spokane Shops. The gondola cars of rock were loaded at the gravel pit west of Bonners Ferry. Jordan Spreader No. X893, directly behind No. 2000, was purchased in 1947 and may be only months old in this image from July 7, 1947.

Extra 2000 East ascends the Shiloh Hill grade just north of Naples, with the William A. Kerstetter ranch and McFarland-Brown Company lumber mill in the background. This 1949 view captures the last remining months of Spokane International steam operations before diesels took over in early October of that year.

The Union Pacific and its subsidiaries bought a total of 362 Mikado, or 2-8-2 wheel arrangement, locomotives. No. 2000 was built in April 1911 for the Oregon-Washington Railroad & Navigation Company as No. 1100. The OWR&N was eventually absorbed into the Oregon Short Line, which renumbered this locomotive as a Class MK-1 No. 2000. In 1947, the Spokane International purchased the engine, seen passing Naples, Idaho, westbound to Spokane.

The Spokane International kept the inherited Union Pacific number designation 1936 for this engine. Built as Class MK-3 No. 536 in October 1912, this locomotive, weighing in at 270,400 pounds, exerted 47,945 pounds of tractive effort at 210 pounds per square inch boiler pressure. The photographer notes, "No. 15 blasts up Shiloh Hill kicking up a storm of smoke and steam for the grade ahead."

Six

BONNERS FERRY

The Alco RS-1 road switcher was released in early 1941 after Electro-Motive Corporation's popular FT cab road locomotive delivered respectable horsepower and incredible maintenance savings. Fred Rummel, the new president of the Spokane International, understood the need to replace ailing motive power and upgrade infrastructure by purchasing 12 RS-1s between 1949 and 1953.

The Spokane International bought a pair of secondhand 2-6-0s and two 4-6-0s in 1906 from the Atlantic Equipment Company. Here, 2-6-0 No. 11, built in 1888, is pictured near Bonners Ferry. This locomotive was used in initial rail line construction and regular service from about 1906 until 1923, when it was sold to the Humbird Lumber Company.

Of the 15 original (1906 to 1954) cabooses, the Spokane International had only two home-built cabooses, Nos. C-4 and C-7. No. C-4 was built in 1914 and appears to be taking up the rear of a maintenance-of-way train with empty flatcars used for rail or crosstie replacement along with steam crane No. 1 somewhere in the Kootenai River valley near Bonners Ferry. (Both, Jerry Quinn collection.)

Promotional literature by American Hoist & Derrick Company advertised that the "American RR Ditcher would build a railroad from stem to stern as a Steam Shovel, Pile Driver, Track Layer, Locomotive Crane, Light Locomotive, Ballast Digger and Spreader." Its versatility allowed track-level operation or operation from a flatcar, as illustrated in this July 1918 Frank Godfrey photograph taken east of Bonners Ferry.

On Sunday, April 13, 1975, a westbound Union Pacific *Business Special* eases across the five-span wooden Howe truss built over the Kootenai River at Bonners Ferry. Railroads periodically run special passenger trains as excursions or for railroad officials and shippers to inspect operations. The Union Pacific Railroad owns one of the largest collections of operating heritage equipment; here, 1960s vintage E9 No. 960 leads the way. (Both, Jerry Quinn collection.)

Crossing the Kootenai River at 10–15 miles per hour, the engineer on No. 103 cautiously watches a sprinkler behind the rear driver wheel misting water on ties and the wooden Howe trestle to prevent a disastrous fire. At times, steel brake shoes overheated on trains descending steep Moyie Hill, spinning off dangerous red-hot brake shoe shavings in the bone-dry days of August. (Walter Ainsworth collection, PNRArchive.org.)

Spokane International Nos. 200 and 201 were the only Alco RS-1s with steam generators and the distinctive additional automobile headlight over the number board. After passenger train service was discontinued in September 1954, the SI introduced a fast freight service with a baggage/mail car. Here, No. 201 leads Train No. 9 across the Kootenai River bridge.

The Selkirk Mountains form a backdrop for a view of the systemwide September 1995 Union Pacific 18-car business train just west of Schnoors, near Bonners Ferry. Powering the train are locomotives Nos. 951, 949, and 963B—the last of Union Pacific's high-speed diesel-electrics built for service on the famous streamliner and domeliner passenger trains. (Gary & Roz Miller, Jerry Quinn collection.)

Three of the Alco RS-1s switch a lumber mill just west of downtown Bonners Ferry. The carcasses of old trucks and remnants of other equipment reveal the tenacity that many independent logging/lumber mills in northern Idaho exhibited to keep their businesses profitable in a competitive marketplace.

The Great Northern entered Bonners Ferry in 1892, with Jim Hill building north to Kuskonook, British Columbia, impeding Canadian Pacific influence in the region. The GN and SI interchanged at Bonners Ferry with GN's Port Hill branch reaching to the border. The GN assigned older locomotives to the line, and in 1944, No. 219 was the last 4-4-0 in service on the Great Northern. (Maynard Rikerd, Jerry Quinn collection.)

Pulling into Bonners Ferry from Spokane at about 4:00 in the afternoon, Nos. 204 and 205 and two other Alcos ease eastbound Train No. 14 along the double-track line between Schnoors and the Bonners Ferry yard.

The Spokane International was expected to reach Bonners Ferry by Christmas 1905. The arrival was changed to midwinter, as harvest season was winding down, making it difficult to get laborers at $2.50 for a 10-hour day in addition to paying 25¢ for room and board—not too attractive even in 1905. Since 1943, the grain elevators of the General Feed & Grain Company on Third Street have reflected the rich agricultural diversity of the region, including crops of wheat, barley, and hops. The above photograph from 1956 has three SI Alco RS-1s at the Bonners Ferry depot before heading west with Train No. 9. Below, 25 years later in the early 1980s, three Union Pacific SD40-2s and a lone Burlington Northern GE U30-C share the same location. (Below, Harley Kuhel.)

These two Larry Shawver photographs were taken at Bonners Ferry in 1955. Above, combination freight/mail Train No. 9 waits as mail is unloaded at the depot; below, Fast Freight No. 14 sits on the "West" siding near the sawmill ponds. How do railroads designate odd numbers for westbound trains and even numbers for eastbound trains? Traditionally, even-numbered trains (superior) travel east (or north) and odd-numbered trains (inferior) travel west (or south.) Therefore, Train No. 9 above would be westbound to Spokane and No. 14 below would be headed east toward Eastport, Idaho.

The five RS-1s sitting with a westbound train at the Bonners Ferry depot represent nearly half of all 12 diesel locomotives owned by the Spokane International. The photographer's notes about this train read, "Later on in the day this train will cause havoc with the GN main line at Dover . . . when the engineer gives too much throttle and they tear the rails out from under all five engines."

The Alco RS-1 was an early ouster of steam and proved quite successful with many railroads, as its versatility was hard to beat at the time. The long end is the front, mimicking steam locomotives with their long boilers, and the cab provided ample 360-degree visibility. Spokane International No. 211, seen switching in Bonners Ferry, was the last locomotive purchased in August 1953.

In the late 1940s, all railroads in the United States recognized the economic advantages of diesel electric locomotives, with the Spokane International as the first railroad in the Inland Empire to dieselize 100 percent. Fred C. Rummel, a banker and amateur railroader, was the man responsible for the SI's "new look." In April 1949, Rummel ordered nine RS-1 road switchers from the American Locomotive Company (Alco) painted in a most outstanding color scheme. The units were painted black on top and bottom, with yellow trim and a flaming, wide red band through the middle. Above, Sammy Graham is riding No. 208 into Bonners Ferry; below, No. 201 prepares to attack Moyie Hill north of town.

The spectacle of the steam era is captured in this 1949 scene at the Bonners Ferry yard. Former Union Pacific No. 2000 (now SI No. 2000) is getting its fire cleaned while 2-8-0 No. 25 picks up a head of steam to assist an eastbound up Moyie Hill.

The SI 2-8-0s were built by Rogers in 1906 during a period of transition for the steam engine. During the 1920s, master mechanic Charles Prescott considered an extensive rebuilding and upgrade of Nos. 22, 24, and 26 into Nos. 122, 124, and 126 to increase horsepower and efficiency. Not all improvements were accepted, but the distinctive smokebox-mounted Elesco feedwater heater remained.

On a warm summer day in 1955, Spokane International employee Squire Glen walks toward the cab of No. 201 on westbound Train No. 9. The mail/baggage car behind the locomotives may only see a couple of more months of service before the end of mail and express contracts in late 1955.

There were generally three employees needed for the operation of a steam locomotive: the engineer, who is responsible for proper operation of the locomotive; the fireman, who regulates fire and water levels maintaining steam pressure in the boiler; and the hostler, who prepares the engine for service by starting the fire, greasing and oiling, and, as seen here, cleaning or banking the fire.

Occasionally, the Spokane International leased steam engines from neighboring railroads while its motive power was in for repair. In this excellent action scene, Northern Pacific Class W No. 1592 storms upgrade toward Moyie Springs and beyond. Northern Pacific Railway records indicate that this locomotive was leased to the Spokane International from October 20, 1946, through June 1, 1947.

If Train No. 1 is on time at Bonners Ferry, it should be 8:35 a.m. on the Fourth of July 1947. The day started out cool at 43 degrees Fahrenheit and quickly warmed to a high of 81. The No. 101 is one of the four original 4-6-0s built for passenger train service. No. 21, one of the Consolidations (2-8-0), is sitting in the background.

All steam locomotives on the Spokane International were coal-fired with bituminous coal from the Crowsnest region of British Columbia and Alberta, which when burned produced little ash. Here, in a time-honored practice, the hostler is "cleaning" the fire, or shaking the coals in the firebox grate, causing the ash to fall into the ashpan to prevent it from dropping on the wooden trestles.

Of the six freight engines with 2-8-0-wheel arrangements, No. 22 was the first to be rebuilt. Like the 24 and 26 (renumbered 122, 124, and 126), it was given a radical change in appearance with the addition of efficiency-producing Elesco feedwater heaters. A mile or so north of Bonners Ferry, No. 122 passes the grade crossing at Bloom (Blume) Hill Road.

Seven

MOUNTAINS AND TUNNELS

During the building of the Spokane International Railway along the Moyie River north of Bonners Ferry, three tunnels were excavated. The Twohy Brothers contract required cuts through sandhills and boring of two tunnels—one 570 feet long, and the other 375. A jubilant crew exits the southwest portal of sand-faced Tunnel 3 on the front of Baldwin Locomotive Works 2-6-0 No. 11. (Jerry Quinn collection.)

A contemporary of Larry Shawver's, Thomas Kreutz recorded on film many Inland Empire railroads from the late 1940s through the late 1950s. Just a year old, Alco RS-1 No. 201 eases westbound Train No. 1 across the impressive Fry Creek trestle near Bonners Ferry in September 1950. (Tom Kreutz, Washington, Idaho & Montana Railway History Preservation Group collection.)

Flying white flags, though dirty, Extra 2000 East is passing the Fry Creek trestle with an eastbound ore train. In steam and early diesel days, many trains ran on published timetables; any train operating not on a printed schedule was an "extra" train, indicated by white flags (or lights) on the front of the engine.

During initial construction, a mile and a half of track-laying was considered a day's work. This took about four cars of steel and six to eight cars of ties. As ties were laid atop the roadbed, surfacing crews dumped on stone and gravel to hold the ties in place. Track improvements were ongoing; these two images illustrate an example of a line relocation at the Fry Creek trestle. The 1953 SI Annual Report states, "[1952] A large trestle, 489 feet long, at Milepost 113.2, was replaced with an earth fill, and a line change was made by making a deep cut just east of the fill, resulting in the reduction of main line curvature."

The 500-foot rise of elevation in the 10 miles from Bonners Ferry to Moyie Springs creates a one percent eastward grade. Both photographs are near Tunnel No. 3: above, No. 1917 with No. 25 as helper; and below, No. 25 shoves from the rear. Larry Shavwer reminisces, "When climbing Moyie or Shiloh hill, I watched the skill of the engineer as he handled throttle, Johnson bar and sander valve to keep the engine working hard and not lose its footing on the grade, and how the engineer would handle those engines with real skill when they sometimes did slip and lose their footing, especially if the rail was wet, as he had to work fast to get that engine's drivers to take a hold of the rails again and pulling hard."

The Spokane International bought six new cabooses from American Car & Foundry and Haskell & Barker from 1905 to 1910. All original cabooses numbered C-1 through C-8 had wooden underframes. Under normal operating conditions, helpers would need to be coupled in before wooden frame cabooses to prevent them from being crushed by the force of the helper engine. Spokane International cabooses Nos. C-9 through C-16 had steel underframes, permitting helpers to be added behind the caboose. Here are two examples of helper engines cut in before wooden underframe No. C-5. The SI ran helpers facing backwards so they did not need to be turned on a wye for the return trip.

No. 124 (facing backwards) trails an eastbound train passing the Bloom (Blume) Hill grade crossing about six miles north of Bonners Ferry. Former Union Pacific 2-8-2 Mikado No. 1917, built by Baldwin Locomotive Works in 1911 and nearly 40 years old, is running as SI No. 1917 takes the lead in the distance.

In August 1949, Spokane International passenger Train No. 1 travels through northern Idaho with seven Canadian Pacific cattle cars. Livestock originating at Calgary or Lethbridge could still be delivered to Spokane within the United States' 20-hour livestock rest rule. Canadian health regulations for cattle transport specified lime disinfectant sprayed over the inside and lower outside after emptying the car, hence the whitewash color.

The introduction of steam locomotives revolutionized transportation across North America. The mournful wail of the whistle far off in the night, the whoosh of boiler steam, and the welcome warning of "All aboard!" It's all part of the romance of the steam locomotive. Here is a Spokane International engineer's portrayal of a steam engine: "You could feel the power in those little engines and learn the temperament of each of them, as like people, they were all different in their moods. Some of them easy going and willing to work, and others lazy, cantankerous and stubborn, wanting to argue about the matter all the way. The 122 and 124 always seeming to be of a little better disposition than the 126, and the 25 the best of the 20's. The 23 being downright obnoxious, it had to be coaxed on everything until just the right setting of Johnson bar and throttle was found." Here, rear-facing helper No. 126 enters Tunnel No. 1 in 1949.

It's not known for certain what camera Frank Godfrey used in July 1918 to take this unusual image, but it may have been one of Eastman Kodak's new Brownie cameras with roll film. Taking a photograph with a large-format camera while leaning perilously over the top of Tunnel No. 2 with engine No. 25 traveling at 12 miles per hour seems unlikely. (Jerry Quinn collection.)

Union Pacific SD40-2 No. 3334 with westbound Train No. 9 exits Tunnel No. 4 at MP117 in a steep canyon. One observer noted, "When coming out of the tunnel . . . the long drop almost straight down to the Kootenai River, looks so far that if a piece of coal was tossed off the engine it would be around the curve before the coal hit the water." (Harley Kuhel.)

The caption on this print comments, "No. 1 westbound – S.I.'s crack passenger train traveling at speed of 30 miles per hour. Only 42 stops between Eastport and Spokane – 141 miles. July 1918." The exact location is Tunnel Spur near the top of Moyie Hill. The number on the boiler plate is No. 2, renumbered to No. 102 around 1920. (Fred Godfrey, Jerry Quinn Collection)

At Eileen, Idaho, in October 1949, No. 25 is cut off the rear of Train No. 14 after helping up Moyie Hill. The crew repositions the train before returning to "Bonners." Without the helper, it was a challenge to get tonnage of about 2,500 tons up the half-percent grade with an engine rated for about 2,200 tons, but it made it every time.

This July 1948 image at MP126 is a north Idaho railroad town still life. A nearby historical sign summarizes former days: "Meadow Creek emerged to become a center to some 400 loggers, miners, millworkers and stump-farmers. Near the Archer sawmill was a general store-post office, Lazos' Saloon . . . and a dance hall called the Moyie Amusement Club. The fluctuating population gradually declined until the last house was removed in 1975."

The Eastport, Idaho / Kingsgate, British Columbia, port of entry, located south of Yahk, British Columbia, was established in 1906, primarily processing passengers and freight into the mining communities of the East and West Kootenays. The Idaho / British Columbia border is in the shadow on the right. The boxcar in the distance is in British Columbia, with the foreground in Idaho.

In 1955, Spokane International No. 9 arrives at Kingsgate, British Columbia / Eastport, Idaho, about 10:30 in the morning, waiting for clearance and permission to proceed westbound. The combined freight/mail train sits in the warm afternoon sun on the British Columbia side of the border. The US counterpart of Kingsgate, Eastport, Idaho, lies in a deep mountainous valley along the Moyie River.

Photographer Harley Kuehl reminisced about his experiences working for the Union Pacific: "I used to work on the SI/UP after the Milwaukee Road folded up in 1980." One advantage of working for the railroad was to record a westbound/southbound Union Pacific No. 9 at Eastport, Idaho, with three SD40-2s during a mid-1980s snowstorm.

The Spokane International was incorporated to counter Jim Hill's influence in the Inland Empire and to offer a US connection for the Canadian Pacific. Daniel Chase Corbin predicted that when the line was completed, "There will be nothing better than our fast [passenger] trains on the Hill or Harriman roads." The Canadian Pacific initially extended a branch from Curzon on the Nelson-Cranbrook Crowsnest line to Kingsgate, British Columbia. In 1911, the junction was relocated to Yahk, British Columbia, 10.5 miles from the Idaho border at Eastport. These photographs illustrate the SI/CP passenger train connection at Yahk. The crew on Canadian Pacific G5 Class 4-6-2 No. 1204 with CP Train No. 1 greets the crew from Spokane International D1 Class 4-6-0 No. 103 around 1946.

A Rail Diesel Car (RDC) built by the Budd Company of Philadelphia, Pennsylvania, passes through Yahk, British Columbia, in April 1963. These very successful RDCs saved many passenger trains both on main and branch lines, increasing ridership for a time. Budd had a long history of building passenger train equipment; its biggest order (173 passenger cars) equipped the famous Canadian Pacific Railway train *The Canadian*. (Jerry Quinn collection.)

Pictured here about nine miles north of the US/Canadian border near Glenlilly, British Columbia, is F-M "C-Liner" No. 4052. Fairbanks Morse (F-M) diesel locomotives were never very prevalent, with only 66 units produced by the Canadian Locomotive Company (CLC) for Canada-based railroads. Partly due to F-M generator problems, continuing production of the C-liners was impractical without a redesign, and since marketplace acceptance was marginal, their manufacture ended in 1958. (Courtesy Richard Yaremko.)

On September 1, 1981, Nos. 5629, 5635, and 5637—three of the over 450 EMD/GMD SD40-2s Canadian Pacific purchased—pass through Moyie, British Columbia. Part of the Canadian Pacific Railway's revamped corporate image, "CP Rail" colorful freight cars began with the introduction of the "Multimark" theme in 1968. A story is told that the locomotives were originally supposed to be black with a red Multimark (like many freight cars), but when the ad company presented it to CP officials, they said, "We paid you $500,000 to come up with black?" So, the ad company rearranged the colors. The high visibility stripes on the front of many locomotives increased from the original four-inch white stripes to eight-inch stripes in the early 1980s. (Courtesy Richard Yaremko.)

The Canadian Pacific built through the Crowsnest Pass area from Lethbridge, Alberta, to the Continental Divide around 1898. This line was built primarily to access mineral-rich southeastern British Columbia via an all-Canadian rail route, thus asserting Canadian Pacific sovereignty in the area. Above, Mount Hosmer looms over Montreal Locomotive Works (MLW) / Alco No. 4562 with an eastbound empty coal train heading north toward the Elk River coalfields by the Hosmer, British Columbia, station. Below, during the 1970s and 1980s, the railroad was trying to phase out the C-Liners, but periodic shortages of power kept interfering with the plan. Here in September 1973, F-M No. 4057 passes historic Blairmore, Alberta, with an EMD/GMD "B" and "GP" unit and F-M road switcher. (Both, Richard Yaremko.)

On a warm July 1974 day, renowned railroad photographer Richard Yaremko caught these two Canadian Pacific trains stirring up coal dust at the coal tipple in Michel, British Columbia. Daniel Corbin developed coal properties in the Elk River Valley in response to Jim Hill's intrusion into southern British Columbia. The town of Michel was owned by the coal mines, along with the processing plant that converted hard coal to coking coal used to make steel. All this changed in the early 1970s, when Kaiser Resources, the owners of the coal mines, decided to demolish the town and create the new community of Sparwood five miles to the west. This scene has changed, but the CP still moves unit coal trains from the Crowsnest Pass area to the Pacific coast.

No. 4061 is a General Motors Diesel (GMD) FP7A; the "FP" indicates it was operational for freight or passenger service—note the boiler exhaust on the top rear of the locomotive. This Extra West passes the approach signal to Crowsnest, British Columbia, on Saturday, August 4, 1973. The train of lead-zinc concentrate from Pine Point, Northwest Territories, is bound for the Cominco Smelter located at Trail, British Columbia. (Richard Yaremko.)

As the steam era declined and dieselization began in the early 1950s, British Columbia became home to the growing fleet of Fairbanks-Morse (F-M)–designed locomotives built by the Canadian Locomotive Company (CLC). Here, a trio of CLC H-16-44s, with No. 8712 taking the lead, prepares to depart Crowsnest, British Columbia, with eastbound Train No. 72 on Sunday, August 5, 1973. (Courtesy Richard Yaremko.)

At the dawn of the diesel era, manufacturers vied for the attention of North American railroads; among the companies were EMC/EMD, American Locomotive Company (Alco), Baldwin-Lima-Hamilton, and upstart Fairbanks-Morse, which built opposed-piston diesels that worked brilliantly in World War II submarines, but not so well in railroad locomotives. The Canadian Pacific purchased some 65 CLC (F-M) cab-unit (C-Liner) and (H-Series) road switchers. The above image shows H-16-44 No. 8725 and "C-Liner" No. 4104 at Nelson, British Columbia, in April 1974. Below, H-16-44 No. 8555 is switching the Cominco Plant at Trail, British Columbia. A CP dispatcher recalls, "I was working in Montreal, March 11, 1975, on the Pacific Region Railroad Desk, when the order came down to get rid of all the CLC's." C-Liner No. 4104 was saved from the scrapper's torch and resides today in Nelson, British Columbia. (Both, Jerry Quinn collection.)

Eight

LARRY SHAWVER

Larry Shawver, the premier chronicler of the Spokane International, poses on No. 124. In his memoirs, he wrote, "There was a boy, who grew up on a ranch north of Kootenai, Idaho with one corner of the ranch that touched the little line. He had watched and loved trains from the time he was big enough to toddle to the windows as a train went by."

To supplement the aging fleet of steam locomotives and increased freight traffic, three Union Pacific 2-8-0 Mikados were acquired in 1947. They survived a mere two years before the line converted to diesels in 1949–1950. In front of the Sandpoint depot and water tank, No. 1917 steams away on a warm 1949 summer evening.

Larry Shawver notes, "The engine [helper No. 25] would lose its footing . . . there was a fight with throttle and sander valve to get the engine to bite the steel rail again . . . it would feel like hitting a brick wall as the weight of the train slammed back with a sudden speeding up and then slowing down a little so the helper could be cut off."

Historically, most railroads were divided into divisions based on geography and mileage of track; these divisions were further divided into sections. Each section had a section gang assigned, and each section gang had its section house. The section house was basically a toolshed built along the railroad line stocked with tools such as lanterns, shovels, spike mauls, ballast forks, pinch bars, claw bars, track jacks, wrenches for track bolts, track gauges, and other supplies. Most Spokane International sections were between six and ten miles apart. As seen above, railroads were frugal; this section house was converted from SI caboose No. C-3 and located at Petersons Spur / MP66.4 north of Morton. Below, Larry Shawver's father, Truman, is seen sitting at the shelter of flag stop Grouse, rebuilt from caboose No. C-4, on a 1949 summer day.

One goal of a railroad is to get cars in and out of the yard as quickly as possible, just as a tugboat's job is to maneuver ships in the harbor. Switching locomotives generally spent their non-glorious years shuttling cars from here to there. Spokane International switcher 0-6-0 No. 51 was purchased new from Alco in 1910 and worked at Spokane Shops until end of service in 1949.

During the mid-1940s, the SI faced a dilemma of upgrading or replacing its outmoded equipment to keep the railroad running. The most interesting trial was former Akron, Canton & Youngstown 2-8-0 No. 356, which worked the Trentwood Aluminum Plant. Upon inspection, it was found in need of too many repairs and was sent to scrap at Spokane Metals.

In 1956, the Union Pacific informed the Interstate Commerce Commission of its intent to acquire the Spokane International. The Canadian Pacific Railway and other transportation sources contested the matter; after extensive negotiations, the Union Pacific gained total management control in 1959. The UP replaced the Alco RS-1s with EMD-built F-units and GP-9s. Above, F9 No. 505 sits at Spokane Shops, and below, No. 520 leads Train No. 9 at Sandpoint. Larry Shawver expressed his sentiments concerning the new ownership: "There was more character [in the SI] than just another branch of the yellow monster . . .it was a proud little line with a name of its own and a class that could be found nowhere else in any of the other railroads around here."

No. 25 was an Alco 2-8-0 purchased new for the Spokane International in 1906–1907. The 2-8-0 Consolidation was one of the most popular steam locomotives in the early 1900s; one source states, "the 2-8-0 design was the ultimate heavy-freight locomotive. The 2-8-0's forte was starting and moving impressive loads at unimpressive speeds, and its versatility gave the type its longevity." Nearly all the SI Consolidations remained in service until 1949. Larry Shawver recalls a ride on No. 25: "I vividly remember one ride during my first year of high school . . . . There was about three feet of snow on the ground and it had been snowing all day, near Sand Creek Trestle, a train consisting of the plow, No. 25 and a caboose stopped out on the trestle and then backed up. Dan Waite stuck his head out the window and asked me, 'What the hell are you doing here?' 'Going home.' 'Well, get on the engine, you'll never make it this way.' So, I did."

The acronym "Alco," or "ALco," as some locomotive enthusiasts insist, represents the American Locomotive Company. In June 1901, Alco Locomotive Works in Schenectady, New York, began to compete with the impending monopoly of Baldwin Locomotive Works. Hundreds of locomotives were built during the height of the steam era, with Alco's greatest achievement being the largest locomotive ever constructed, the Union Pacific 4-8-8-4 "Big Boy." Alco had been producing diesel locomotives since the 1920s, but it was not until the late 1940s that the company developed one of the most important original road-switcher designs, the RS-1. Spokane International's RS-1 Nos. 200 and 201, purchased in October 1949, were the only two units delivered with steam boilers for passenger train service. Only Nos. 200 and 201 had the unique modified cowcatcher frames with the addition of an automobile-style headlight staring down like a 1950s science-fiction spaceship.

Railroad cabooses became an institution on the rear of freight trains from the 1830s until the end of the 20th century. The Spokane International had 20 cabooses numbered from C-1 to C-16, with some cars being replaced or renumbered. Throughout the years, SI cabooses were painted in various colors; some were "Canadian Pacific maroon," or "boxcar brown." Interestingly, No. C-6 was yellow-orange with black and white lettering for a time around 1940. In later years, nearly all were painted in the distinctive SI diesel colors. The SI bought one caboose from the US Army in 1954, which became No. C-12. Since the late 1980s, no cabooses in regular service trail Union Pacific trains traveling the SI rails, as cabooses have been replaced by "FREDs"—Flashing Rear End Devices.

Bonners Ferry was located between two grades, requiring helpers both ways during the steam era. Freight train crews were changed at Bonners Ferry in both directions until the new yard was built at Kingsgate. The "hill crews" worked the north end trains to Yahk, British Columbia, and back to Bonners Ferry. Opening the CP interchange at Kingsgate eliminated the need for this second crew. In the above image, Nos. 211 and 206 switch a train near the various buildings on the south end of the Bonners Ferry yard. Below, in 1949, No. 2000 in a cloud of sander dust hustles a train of ore east (north) out of Bonners Ferry.

Larry Shawver captioned this photograph, "Sunny side, fast action, and a steam engine. Perfect. 1949." What makes a "perfect" photograph? Whether people are consciously aware or not, one of the main rules in art and photo composition stems from the theory that the human eye naturally gravitates to intersection points that occur when an image is split into thirds. The rule of thirds is an imaginary tic-tac-toe board drawn across an image to break it into nine equal squares. In this image, engineer Tony Sciola is the center of this invisible checkerboard. The shadow of the locomotive indicates the time of day, about midmorning—high noon images are bland, as shadows are needed to create dimension. Of course, a photograph of a steam engine without smoke would seem strange. Spokane International No. 2000 heading up Shiloh Hill with a full head of steam at Selle on a warm 1949 sunny day is indeed a "perfect" steam train portrait.

In the waning days of steam on the Spokane International, Train No. 1 passes ore Extra 122 East at Milltown in Sandpoint. The entire SI steam fleet would not make it through the end of 1949, when diesels started taking control in late autumn. Passenger locomotive 4-6-0 No. 104 would not see service to the end, as it was damaged beyond repair in an accident near Bonners Ferry on July 27, 1949. There was a spot at the North Bonners crossing (Myers Crossing) where people liked to load and unload heavy equipment. They would back a lowboy trailer or truck into the dirt bank along the track and then drive the machinery onto the truck or trailer. It appears that Train No. 1 led by No. 104 hit Mary Wendel's bulldozer, causing a mishap. She sued the SI over the accident and lost—she had to pay the railroad.

Larry Shawver recalls, "Getting a camera as a graduation present, I was ready and eager to start getting pictures. The camera was an old Ansco Royal size 116, with a 1/100 shutter speed and a f7.9 lens . . . the old camera wasn't much, but it was about as good as the average railfan had in those days." In May 1946, an eastbound freight crosses Sand Creek trestle.

With just a three-car train led by a 1907 vintage 4-6-0 locomotive and tailing a cattle car, this August 1949 SI Train No. 1 at Shiloh looks like a short line. The Spokane International may have been only a few hundred miles in length, but most years it met the minimum operating revenue of $1 million to be considered a Class I railroad.

Most Spokane International steam locomotives received modernization and efficiency improvements through the years. This 2-8-0 built by Alco in 1907 was originally No. 26, with that number changed to No. 126 when the engine was rebuilt at the SI's Spokane Shops in 1927. Some of the noticeable changes were larger cylinders and the unique Elesco feedwater heater. No. 126 is pictured here at Sandpoint in June 1946.

Extra No. 21 West tops the Pack River grade near Forest Siding, Idaho, on July 26, 1942. A noteworthy feature is the old arc lamp headlight. Locomotive electric carbon arc lights replaced the archaic, dim oil and acetylene headlights. Some railroad officials considered carbon arc lights unsafe, as they temporarily blinded engineers in oncoming trains. No. 21 was the only locomotive carrying arc lights into the 1940s.

Fred C. Rummel replaced Edgar S. McPherson as Spokane International president in 1948. Anticipating the addition of diesel locomotives, in the summer of 1949, Rummel installed a diesel fueling station at Spokane Shop and converted the machine shop for diesel work. In the fall, he got rid of the rest of the obsolete Spokane Shop property, including the coal dock track, coal conveyor, and other steam engine maintenance equipment. He tore down this coaling station at North Bonners and installed diesel fueling services at Bonners Ferry. The official report states, "The facility at North Bonners is no longer necessary on account of diesel locomotive operation." Here, No. 124 rests at the North Bonners Ferry coal dock in May 1949, just months before it was dismantled.

In July 1949, Al Parsons does bell repair on No. 25 at Eileen, north of Bonners Ferry. Parsons was an engineer on the Spokane International during the Roaring Twenties. Larry Shawver relates, "This period brought about many amusing stories of incidents that happened in the liquor running trade on the line and the arrest of a few of the trainmen." Parsons wanted no part of it; he would stay in the engine or caboose while they were unloading the booze. The whisky would be stashed in coal-filled boxcars or buried in coal gondolas loaded near the Fernie, British Columbia, mines. The SI picked up the cars at Yahk and brought them across the border. Longtime SI employee Dewey Almas admitted, "We would help them [bootleggers] dig it out of the coal and unload anywhere from 150 to 400 cases. . . . The bootleggers would give us a case of whisky, sometimes two, for each man."

Former Union Pacific 2-8-2 No. 1917 with an eastbound train waits at the west approach of the Kootenai River bridge in Bonners Ferry. No. 2000 in the background has just pushed mangled passenger engine 4-6-0 No. 104 down Moyie Hill into town after it hit a truck loading a bulldozer blocking the tracks in July 1949.

The Spokane International became power short during World War II. Four well-used Delaware & Hudson 2-8-0s were purchased in April 1943. Notable is the wide "ugly duckling" Wootten firebox designed to burn less inexpensive culm, or small pieces of anthracite coal. The locomotive was originally a "camelback," with the cab in the middle, as it was impractical to mount the cab behind the very wide firebox. It was rebuilt around 1930.

Spokane International bought this Standard Type 2-200 Jordan Spreader-Ditcher-Snowplow new in 1947. The O.F. Jordan Company used the slogan "Does the Work of an Army of Men." Advertising literature of the era touted, "The Jordan flanges and bucks snow in one operation. Its rugged manganese cutting blades rip out accumulated ice and packed snow below the top of the rail." This was perfect for Inland Empire winters.

The caboose roster for the Spokane International was constant, with Nos. C-1 thru C-7 from 1905 through May 1942, with the purchase of No. 102 from the Ohio Match Company–Burnt Cabin Railroad. Adding this caboose as No. C-8 required removal of the side door. It was painted "boxcar brown" until around 1949, when it was changed to the diesel-era red-and-black scheme.

An endearing piece of equipment, even to the public, the caboose was an all-too-common sight that many folks anticipated watching as the end of the train went by. To many, a caboose was not a caboose without a cupola. Crewmen in the cupola could better watch the rear of the train for both possible derailments and a train coming up from behind; a rear brakeman was also assigned to the car. Despite improvements, human error can have tragic consequences. On the night of July 27, 1949, sixty-three-year-old conductor George A. Hopkins, here pictured on caboose No. C-6, died on a stalled ore extra east after refusing the wishes of the rear brakeman to put out a red fuse warning a following train. Unfortunately, shortly thereafter, the caboose was rear-ended at Meadow Creek, Idaho.

The humble words of Larry Shawver complete the Spokane International story: "I never considered myself a photographer and my pictures were taken for my own pleasure, but enclosed are some for your consideration. The pictures shall speak for themselves. In looking them over and considering the adverse North Idaho weather conditions much of the time and the poles that the SI had setting so close to the tracks that were always on the sunny side if the sun was shining . . . and last but not least, the most important of all, the camera they were taken with. I am not trying to alibi for them and I know that they are poor pictures, leaving much to be desired, but to me they are part of a priceless collection, one that I worked so hard on for many years. But in my opinion, the award of getting them was well worth the effort." Pictured is Spokane International (Union Pacific) Milepost 44 near Athol, Idaho. (Jerry Quinn.)

Visit us at
arcadiapublishing.com

www.ingramcontent.com/pod-product-compliance
Lightning Source LLC
Chambersburg PA
CBHW060938170426
43194CB00027B/2992